Essential Physical Science

LIGHT AND SOUND

Louise and Richard Spilsbury

Raintree is an imprint of Capstone Global Library Limited, a company incorporated in England and Wales having its registered office at 7 Pilgrim Street, London, EC4V 6LB – Registered company number: 6695582

www.raintreepublishers.co.uk
myorders@raintreepublishers.co.uk

Text © Capstone Global Library Limited 2014
First published in hardback in 2014
Paperback edition first published in 2015
The moral rights of the proprietor have been asserted.

Edited by Nancy Dickmann, Adam Miller, and Diyan Leake
Designed by Victoria Allen
Original illustrations © Capstone Global Library Ltd 2013
Illustrated by H L Studios
Picture research by Ruth Blair
Originated by Capstone Global Library Ltd
Printed and bound in China by CTPS

ISBN 978 1 406 25991 9 (hardback)
17 16 15 14 13
10 9 8 7 6 5 4 3 2 1

ISBN 978 1 406 26001 4 (paperback)
18 17 16 15 14
10 9 8 7 6 5 4 3 2 1

British Library Cataloguing in Publication Data
Spilsbury, Louise.
  Light and sound. -- (Essential physical science)
  1. Light--Juvenile literature. 2. Sound--Juvenile literature.
  I. Title II. Series III. Spilsbury, Richard, 1963-
  534-dc23

Acknowledgements
We would like to thank the following for permission to reproduce photographs: Alamy pp. 8 (© GIPhotoStock X), 15 (© Arcaid Images), 31 (© AfriPics.com), 34 (© Arco Images GmbH), 38 (© Papilio), 39 (© Simon Belcher), 41 (© BSIP SA), 42 (© Horizon International Images Limited); Capstone Publishers (© Karon Dubke) pp. 12, 13, 18, 19, 36, 37; Corbis pp. 17 (© Joana Toro/dpa), 21 (© Norbert Wu/Science Faction); Getty Images pp. 9 (Ian Gavan), 23 (Joel Sartore/National Geographic), 25 (Datacraft Co. Ltd), 29 (Dimitri Vervitsiotis), 40 (Visuals Unlimited, Inc./GIPhotoStock); © Anish Kapoor. All Rights Reserved, DACS 2012 p. 26 (Shutterstock/© gary718); Science Photo Library pp. 6 (Andrew Lambert Photography), 11 (NASA); Shutterstock pp. 4 (© egd), 5 (© WindImage), 7 (© Steve Mann), 10 (© melissaf84), 22 (© Monkey Business Images), 24 (© Angelo Gilardelli), 28 (© MilanB), 33 (© Dmitry Naumov), 35 (© ssuaphotos), 43 (© oorka).

Cover photograph of a trombonist at a festival reproduced with permission of Superstock (Cosmo Condina).

Every effort has been made to contact copyright holders of material reproduced in this book. Any omissions will be rectified in subsequent printings if notice is given to the publisher.

Disclaimer
All the internet addresses (URLs) given in this book were valid at the time of going to press. However, due to the dynamic nature of the internet, some addresses may have changed, or sites may have changed or ceased to exist since publication. While the author and publisher regret any inconvenience this may cause readers, no responsibility for any such changes can be accepted by either the author or the publisher.

Contents

Eureka moment!

Learn about important discoveries that have brought about further knowledge and understanding.

DID YOU KNOW?

Discover fascinating facts about light and sound.

WHAT'S NEXT?

Read about the latest research and advances in essential physical science.

Some words are shown in bold, **like this**. You can find out what they mean by looking in the glossary.

What are light and sound?

Light and sound are essential to our lives. What would a firework display be like without loud bangs, screaming whistles, and brightly coloured lights? Sound and light help us to enjoy and to understand the world around us. They help us to work, play, communicate, and escape danger. Emergency sirens, such as tornado sirens, are loud, noise-making devices that can warn a whole town about a threat.

Sirens and flashing lights give a clear signal to nearby traffic and pedestrians to pull over and allow police, ambulances, or other emergency vehicles to pass quickly and safely.

Eureka moment!

Steam whistles were an early form of siren. As from the 1830s, they were used to send signals on trains and in factories. Steam whistles were also used in lighthouses to warn ships at sea of nearby rocks or hazards.

Forms of energy

Sound and light are forms of **energy**. Energy is the ability or power to make things work or happen. Energy can be carried from one place to another. Sunlight is a type of energy that moves from the Sun to the Earth. When we speak, the sounds we make are a type of energy that moves from our mouths to people's ears.

Burning gunpowder explodes with a loud banging sound, and sends fireworks into the air. Different metals in the gunpowder burn and glow in different colours to create the light displays we see.

How do we make sounds?

Sounds happen when things **vibrate**. When something vibrates, it moves backwards and forwards or up and down very quickly. This is what happens to the surface of a drum when it is hit with a drumstick. When something vibrates, it makes the air around it vibrate, too. The vibrating air carries the sounds people hear. That's why we stop hearing the sound of a drum when the drummer puts a hand on its surface to stop it vibrating.

Feel the vibrations that sounds make by touching your throat when you hum. You can actually see vibrations by putting grains of rice on a drum before you hit it.

Eureka moment!

In 1876, Alexander Graham Bell invented the telephone. When he spoke into his new machine, it changed sound vibrations into **electric currents** that travelled down a wire. At the other end of the wire, the electric currents were changed back into sound vibrations, so his voice could be heard.

How do sounds move?

Sound vibrations travel in invisible patterns called **sound waves**. The waves spread out from a source in all directions, like ripples when you drop a stone in water. Sound waves spread out and pass through gaps or around obstacles, which is why we can hear around corners! When we whisper to someone, we cup our hands around our mouth. This makes a funnel, or cone shape, that helps to focus some of the sound energy in one direction, towards the listener.

DID YOU KNOW?

The speed of sound is about 1,236 kilometres (768 miles) per hour in the air, also known as Mach 1. The word *supersonic* means "faster than the speed of sound". A plane travelling through the sky at supersonic speed creates a sonic boom, which sounds like a loud explosion on the ground.

Constant noise from aeroplanes flying over houses near airports can affect residents' sleep, work, and concentration.

Loud and soft

The loudness or softness of sounds depend on the energy in the vibrations. Things that vibrate a lot make a lot of noise! When you hit a drum really hard, you make bigger, stronger vibrations and louder sounds. When you tap a drum or pluck a guitar string gently, you make smaller, weaker vibrations and softer sounds. The further away you are from a sound, the quieter it gets. This is because sound loses energy as it travels.

Sound waves get taller

Turn up the volume! When you start to hit a drum harder, the vibrations get bigger, the sound waves get taller, and the sounds get louder.

DID YOU KNOW?

One of the loudest natural sounds ever heard came from the eruption of the volcano Krakatoa in Indonesia in 1883. A witness said the explosion still sounded like cannon-fire when it reached him almost 5,000 kilometres (3,100 miles) away. That's like people in London clearly hearing an explosion that happened in Baltimore in the United States.

Reflecting and absorbing

The space in which a sound is made affects the way it moves, too. Sound waves **reflect**, or bounce off, hard, flat surfaces. That's why we hear **echoes** sometimes, when sound waves reflect back to us from a surface. Soft, bumpy surfaces **absorb** sound waves. Sounds in a room that has carpets, soft seats, and curtains will be different from sounds in an empty room with a wooden floor.

DID YOU KNOW?

The way sound travels in a room is called **acoustics**. Without any echoes in a concert hall, music sounds flat. If there are too many echoes, the music sounds fuzzy. Concert halls are built in special shapes and equipped with panels of different sizes and textures to absorb or reflect sounds to create the best acoustics for the audience.

What do sounds travel through?

Most of the sounds we hear come to us through the air around us. We may not be able to see air, but air is a **medium** – a material through which sound waves can travel. Sound travels through other mediums, too. It can travel through solids such as metal, stone, and wood, and through liquids such as water.

Sound vibrations travel faster through some mediums than others. For example, sound travels faster through wood than through air. If you get a friend to tap a desk and listen with your head against the desk, the noise will sound louder than it does when you listen in the air.

Sound is an effective way for whales to communicate across deep, dark oceans where they cannot see each other. Blue whales make sounds that can be heard by other whales that are over 800 kilometres (500 miles) away.

DID YOU KNOW?

Sound travels four times faster through water than through air, and 15 times faster through steel than through air.

Sounds in space

Sound always needs a medium to travel through. Sound cannot travel through a **vacuum** – a completely empty space that has nothing in it, not even air. Space is not a perfect vacuum, but there is far too little air in it for sound vibrations to travel through. That's why astronauts can see but not hear each other when they are outside a spacecraft in space.

Eureka moment!

In 1660, the English scientist Robert Boyle discovered that sound waves can only travel if they have a medium to move through. He put an alarm clock in a jar, then pumped out all the air from the jar. As he could no longer hear the alarm ringing, he'd proved that sound needs a medium to travel through.

Astronauts on a space walk need to wear special suits to survive. Even if they did not, they still could not talk or hear each other without radios because in space there is not enough medium to carry the sound waves.

Try this!

Test three different materials to see how they affect loudness and sound quality (whether sounds are clear or fuzzy).

Prediction

Firmer materials reflect sound better than softer ones.

What you need

- a cardboard box with one open end (ideally over approximately 30 × 30 centimetres (1 × 1 foot))
- tape (preferably the easy-peel type)
- Kraft paper or wallpaper
- felt, or some other thick fabric
- sponges or pads of foam
- scissors

What you do

1 Think of the cardboard box as a room with three walls, a ceiling, and a floor. Get a friend to speak into the open end of the box while you listen behind the other (closed) end of the box. In a normal speaking voice, say, "Hello, how clear and loud does my voice sound now?" to your partner. Swap places and repeat this. Both of you should listen carefully.

2 Cut the paper into three pieces and stick these to the three inside "walls" of the box with tape, to represent wallpaper. Repeat the speaking sound test that you did in step 1. Is the sound quality and volume different to when there was no paper on the walls of the box? Remove the paper and listen again in the "empty" room.

3 Cut the fabric or felt into three pieces and stick these on the three sides of the box to represent curtains. Try the speaking test again. Do curtains make more difference to the noise level than paper?

4 Tape the sponges to the three sides of the box. These represent sound-absorbing panels. Try the speaking test again. Compare the sound quality and volume to when there were no absorbing panels.

Conclusion

You should have found that paper reflects sound better than the softer materials. Which of the softer materials you tested absorbed most sound? This was the one in which sounds were softest and fuzziest. Can you think of other materials that would make sounds louder and clearer?

How do we hear sounds?

To hear sounds, our ears detect vibrations made by sound waves. The outer part of the ear acts as a funnel to direct sound waves into the ear. Here they hit a thin sheet of skin called the eardrum. The sound waves make the eardrum vibrate in a similar way to the original source of the vibration. The eardrum makes three tiny bones (called ossicles) vibrate. These increase the vibrations and pass them into a tube called the cochlea. **Nerves** in the cochlea change vibrations into electrical signals that go to the brain, and we hear the sound. This all happens very quickly.

nerves send signals to brain

ossicles

outer ear

Sound vibrations make parts of our ears vibrate so we can hear many different sounds.

eardrum

DID YOU KNOW?

You have two ears to tell you which direction sound comes from. The one closest to the sound hears it a bit before and a bit louder than the other. The brain uses this difference to work out where sounds come from.

Sound signals

The cochlea is lined with 30,000 tiny nerves called hair cells, which look like miniscule hairs. Each hair cell picks up and codes different sounds. People may suffer hearing loss when cochlea hair cells get damaged. For example, very loud sounds can cause vibrations that hit the hair cells so hard they bend or break. Hearing aids called cochlear implants can help people to hear better by changing sounds into electrical signals for them.

Deaf musicians can use sound vibrations to play instruments. Evelyn Glennie removes her boots to make it easier for her to feel the vibrations from her instruments.

WHAT'S NEXT?

A new metal collar may help deaf people enjoy music. It picks up sound vibrations and transmits them directly into a person's skin. This triggers the same sound-processing brain regions as in those with full hearing.

How are high and low sounds made?

We know that loud and quiet sounds are produced by large or small vibrations, but what about high or low sounds, such as a whistle or a lion's roar? High or low sounds are made by fast or slow vibrations. The number of vibrations per second is called the **frequency** of the sound. If you stand on a beach and three waves pass you in a second, the frequency of those waves is three per second. With sound waves, the more frequently or faster something vibrates, the higher the sound it makes.

Eureka moment!

In around 1600, the Italian scientist Galileo discovered that the frequency of sound waves changes how high or low they sound. He noticed that the spacing of the grooves made by a chisel on a brass plate made the sounds of the chisel scraping over it higher or lower.

The low sound of a bass guitar has a low frequency. The high sound of a whistle has a high frequency. The distance between the top of one wave and another is called its **wavelength**.

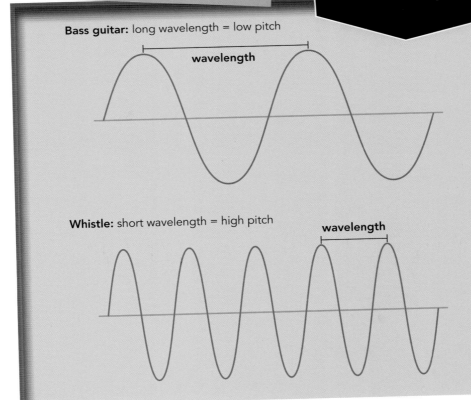

Bass guitar: long wavelength = low pitch

wavelength

Whistle: short wavelength = high pitch

wavelength

Higher and lower

Musicians use the word **pitch** to describe frequency. When the length of a guitar string is changed, it vibrates at a different frequency. A long string gives a lower frequency and pitch. Pressing a finger on it can shorten a string. Shorter strings have a higher frequency and pitch. Blowing into a recorder makes the column of air inside it vibrate and produce sounds. When you put fingers over the holes in a recorder, you change the length of the column of air. The shorter the length of the column of air, the higher the frequency.

DID YOU KNOW?

Young people hear a wider variety of noises than adults. Some ring-tones play at such a high pitch that people over the age of 20 cannot hear them!

The longer bars of the marimba make lower notes than the short ones.

Investigate how the pitch of a note changes as you change the string's length and tightness.

What you need

- a large, empty can
- a hook
- modelling clay
- a ruler
- thin elastic
- a plastic bottle
- weights (small enough to fit inside the bottle, such as marbles)

What you do

1 Push or hammer the hook into the lid of the can, near one edge.

2 Use the modelling clay to attach the ruler to the opposite edge of the can. It should be standing on one of its short edges.

3 Cut a strip of elastic about a metre (3 feet) long. Tie one end around the hook and the other to the top of the plastic bottle. Stand the tin near the edge of a table, put a weight into the bottle and hang it over the edge of the ruler.

4 Pluck the elastic (this is like the string of your instrument) with your finger. Listen carefully to the note it makes and how high or low it sounds.

5 Put another weight into the bottle and pluck the string again. What difference does this make? Try this a few more times. How does the note change as the string gets longer and tighter?

Conclusion

Looser strings make lower notes. When weights pull on the string, they tighten it. Tightening a string gives it a higher pitch (or frequency), while loosening it lowers the frequency. When string players tighten or loosen their strings, they are altering the pitches to make them in tune.

Stay safe!
Make sure the tin doesn't have any jagged edges that could scratch you, and don't pluck the elastic too hard in case it flicks up and hits you in the eye.

How do we use sound?

Sound is used in many ways in science and industry. **Sonar** devices are used to find and locate objects under the sea. Sonar machines send out sound waves. When the waves hit an object, echoes are reflected off it. The machine then analyses the echoes. By working out the direction of returning echoes and measuring the time taken for them to return, the sonar machine can give precise information about the direction, size, and position of the object.

The word *sonar* is an abbreviation for *sound*, *navigation*, and *ranging*. People use sonar to map the shape and features of the ocean floor.

ship

sonar receiver

sonar transmitter

sound waves

sound waves

submarine

Eureka moment!

Lewis Nixon invented the very first sonar-type listening device in 1906, as a way for ships to detect icebergs.

Using sonar

Sonar has many uses. Fishing boats use sonar equipment to locate schools of fish. Naval ships detect enemy submarines and mines using sonar. Sonar can also be used to find shipwrecks and to measure water depths. Some scientists use sonar to explore under ground. They send sound waves into the ground. Then they study the echoes that reflect off layers of rock under ground to identify those that might be worth drilling into to find useful gas, oil, or other **minerals**.

DID YOU KNOW?

Dolphins and porpoises use a type of sonar called **echolocation** to find animals to eat. They send out high-frequency sounds and then use the echoes from possible prey to work out their type, location, speed, and direction of movement.

As the fan-shaped sonar beam scans a given area bit by bit, it creates different coloured points that represent the time of each echo return. These are used to plot a line on a screen. The different colours show the strengths of the different returning echoes.

Ultrasound machines

Doctors in hospitals use a special kind of sonar equipment called **ultrasound**. An ultrasound machine uses sound waves of a very high frequency that produces different echoes when reflected by different **organs** inside the body, such as the heart and liver. Doctors can use these echoes to detect cancer **tumours**, and diseases such as liver disease. Doctors also use ultrasound to scan unborn babies inside their mother's body, so they can monitor the babies' growth and health.

WHAT'S NEXT?

In the future, hospitals may be equipped with ultrasound devices that produce highly focused sound waves. These can be used to break up blood clots in the brain or destroy diseased brain tissue without the need for surgery or drugs.

Doctors and nurses move a handheld ultrasound device over a pregnant woman's stomach. This sends and receives sound waves which a computer compares and converts into an image of the baby on a monitor.

Ultrasonic waves

Since the 1950s, ultrasonic waves have been used to clean delicate machinery parts – for example, to dislodge very tiny bits of dirt or other matter from aircraft. Today, ultrasound is also used to clean objects such as watches and jewellery. Manufacturers use ultrasonic waves to test the quality of metals, plastics, and other materials in the things they make. Some dentists use ultrasonic waves to clean teeth – and nowadays you can even buy ultrasonic toothbrushes!

DID YOU KNOW?

Bats use ultrasound to hunt prey. The sound waves they produce are very close together, so they can detect the very small prey that they prefer, such as moths. Dolphins make waves further apart to find larger prey, including fish.

How does light move?

Light is similar to sound in some ways. Light and sound are both forms of energy, and they both carry energy in the form of waves. Like sound, light moves in waves away from its source. However, unlike sound, light tries to move in straight lines that we call **rays**.

An object that gives off light – for example, the Sun, a lamp, or a computer screen – is **luminous**. The Sun is our most important natural source of light. We manufacture most of the other luminous objects we use. A torch bulb glows because electricity heats a wire inside it, and a candle gives off light as its wick burns.

When a cloud moves in front of the Sun in the sky, we can sometimes see rays of sunlight shining from behind.

WHAT'S NEXT?

Scientists are working on "living lamps" made of glass jars filled with **bacteria** that give off a green glow when fed with methane gas. Methane is produced by rotting household waste – so, one day we could have natural light in our homes and reduce waste at the same time!

Transparent and opaque

Unlike sound, light waves can move through a vacuum. That is why sunlight can travel through space from the Sun to Earth. However, light cannot move through everything. Light can move through transparent material, such as glass, air, and water, but it cannot pass through **opaque** things, such as walls, trees, and us! When opaque materials stop light passing through them, shadows form on the other side of them, where the light cannot reach. Some things are translucent – for example, the **lenses** in dark glasses. Translucent materials let some, but not all, of the light to pass through them.

▷ DID YOU KNOW?

Light moves faster than anything else in the Universe. Light is a million times faster than sound. Light from the Sun takes only 8 minutes to travel 150 million kilometres (93 million miles) to Earth. This means that we see the sunset 8 minutes after it actually happened.

The tennis player casts a shadow in bright sunlight but the shadow of the racket head is lighter than other parts. This is because although the strings are opaque, light shines through holes between them.

Reflecting and absorbing light

When light cannot pass through an object, it reacts in different ways. Some of the waves are reflected, or bounce back off the surface of the object. Some waves are absorbed. Dark surfaces absorb more light than they reflect and light surfaces reflect more light than they absorb. Smooth, flat surfaces reflect light best. When light hits a mirror or the metal roof of a car, its rays bounce off in only one direction, like a bouncing ball.

Mirrors reflect light efficiently because they are very smooth and shiny.

DID YOU KNOW?

There is no such thing as moonlight! Only stars, such as our Sun, are luminous and make light. The light of the Moon is actually a reflection of the light from the Sun. So on a moonlit night, we're actually getting sunlight that's bouncing off the Moon.

Scattering light

Most surfaces are not completely smooth and flat when you look at them up close. When light shines on a surface such as a tree or concrete, its waves bounce off in lots of different directions. This is called **scattering**. Scattering is how sunlight lights up the Earth. When waves of sunlight hit tiny **particles** of dust in the **atmosphere**, the light is scattered in all directions so that its light spreads all around. It's dark in space because there is no atmosphere there to scatter light from the stars.

WHAT'S NEXT?

In the future, we may be able to buy invisibility cloaks! Scientists are developing thin, film-like materials that can interrupt the flow of light and channel it around objects rather than being absorbed or reflected by it. This will make the object appear invisible.

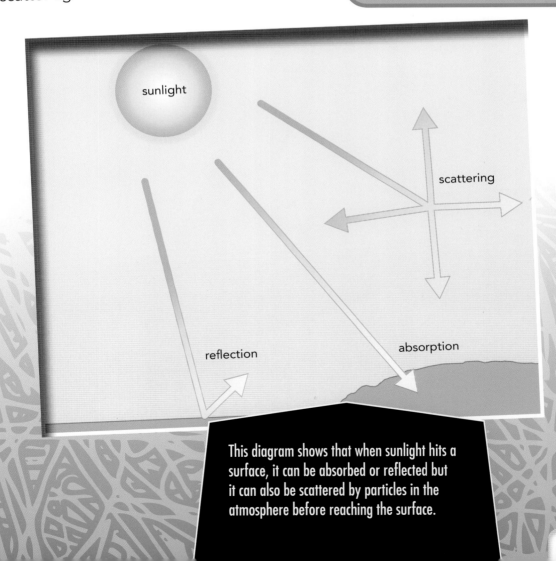

sunlight

scattering

reflection

absorption

This diagram shows that when sunlight hits a surface, it can be absorbed or reflected but it can also be scattered by particles in the atmosphere before reaching the surface.

Refraction

Light can also bend. Have you ever noticed how a straw looks bent in a glass of water, or how a swimming pool looks shallower than it really is? These effects are caused by **refraction**, which is the way light bends when it passes through something. Refraction happens because light travels at different speeds through different things. It moves faster through air than water. Light slows down by about 25 per cent when it moves from air to water. As it slows down, it changes its direction – it bends, or refracts.

The straw looks bent because light slows down when it moves from air to water.

Moving through mediums

Light, like sound, can travel through different mediums. When light shines into glass, water, or plastic, it also refracts. The amount the light bends depends on the type of medium it travels through. For example, light moves more slowly through glass than through water, so light refracts more when moving through glass than when moving through water.

DID YOU KNOW?
Archer fish use their mouth like a water pistol, shooting water out to knock insects off branches into the water. To aim accurately, they have to allow for refraction, and have learned that there is less distortion of their vision of the target if they position themselves directly beneath it.

When light hits a diamond, some of it reflects back but some travels into the centre of the diamond and bounces around inside before finally escaping. This makes the diamond sparkle.

How does light help us to see?

We can only see because of light. We see when light reflects off an object and enters our eyes. Light enters the eye through the black spot in the middle called the pupil. It passes through a cornea and a lens, which both help to focus light on to the **retina** at the back of the eyeball. The retina is covered in nerve cells that send signals down the optic nerve to the brain. The brain turns these signals into the image that we see.

The image passed to the retina is upside-down. The brain turns it the right way up again.

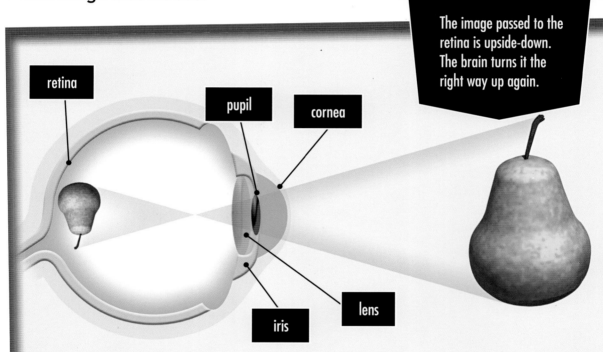

retina

pupil

cornea

lens

iris

WHAT'S NEXT?

A new, artificial retina could help blind people to see. A video camera in a pair of glasses records scenes and sends beams of light on to a computer chip at the back of the eyeball. This creates electrical signals that pass directly into the optic nerve.

Changing light

Our eyes are constantly changing to control how much light gets into them and to focus on different things. The **iris**, the coloured part of the eye, is a circle of muscle that changes the size of the pupil. In bright light, eyes need to take in less light to be able to see, so it makes the pupil smaller. In low light, it makes the pupil bigger, to take in more light. Other muscles change the shape of the lens to make it focus on things near and far.

Cats' eyes seem to glow when light shines on them. This is because they reflect light inside to help them see!

DID YOU KNOW?

Cats can see in low light because of a mirror-like part at the back of their eyes called the *tapetum lucidum*. This reflects any light that is not absorbed by the retina. The reflected light is bounced back so the retina has another chance to absorb it.

How do glasses help us see?

People who are short-sighted cannot see things at a distance clearly. Their lenses focus the image in front of the retina. People who are long-sighted see things far away clearly, but their near vision is blurry. Their lenses focus the image behind the retina. Some people wear glasses to help them see more clearly if the lenses in their eyes do not refract light on to the retina properly. The lenses in glasses are curved in order to refract light so it hits the retina again.

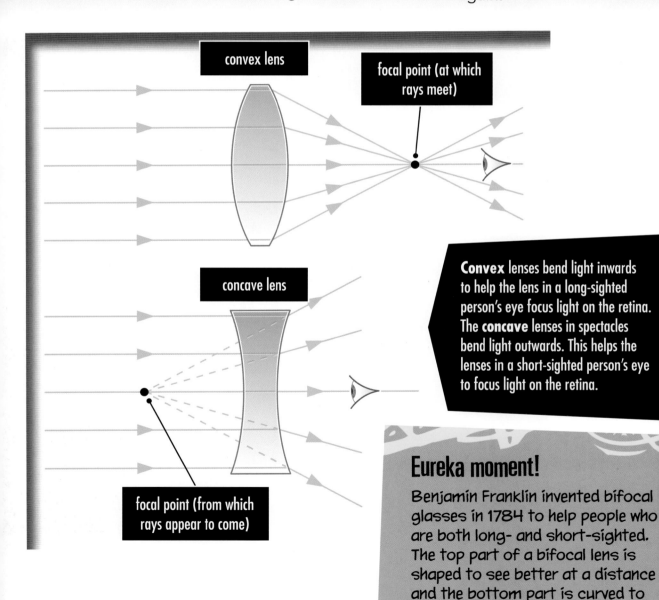

convex lens

focal point (at which rays meet)

concave lens

focal point (from which rays appear to come)

Convex lenses bend light inwards to help the lens in a long-sighted person's eye focus light on the retina. The **concave** lenses in spectacles bend light outwards. This helps the lenses in a short-sighted person's eye to focus light on the retina.

Eureka moment!

Benjamin Franklin invented bifocal glasses in 1784 to help people who are both long- and short-sighted. The top part of a bifocal lens is shaped to see better at a distance and the bottom part is curved to see better up close.

Contact lenses

Contact lenses are also curved lenses that refract light to help people see, worn directly on the surface of the eye. Tears on the surface of the eyes help to hold them in place. A Swiss doctor called Adolf Fick made the first contact lenses in 1887 from glass. They were large and heavy, and they covered the entire eye surface, so they were very uncomfortable to wear! Today's contact lenses are made from thin, soft, flexible plastic and only cover the iris, so wearers cannot feel them.

In order to see well, light has to be perfectly focused on a person's retina. Glasses and contact lenses refract light so that it hits a person's retina correctly.

DID YOU KNOW?

The newest thing in contact lenses is a special liquid substance, with a person's lens prescription, that can be sprayed on to the eye. It hardens into a contact lens that lasts for up to 24 hours.

How do we see colours?

Light seems to be colourless, but in fact it is made up of different coloured waves. Each colour has a different wavelength. For example, violet light has a shorter wavelength than red light. Objects are a particular colour when they reflect one wavelength and absorb others. For example, a ripe tomato looks bright red because its skin reflects the red light in sunlight and absorbs all other colours. An object appears black when it absorbs all wavelengths, and white when it reflects all wavelengths.

When light waves pass through water droplets which have many sides, it splits into its different colours: red, orange, yellow, green, blue, indigo, and violet.

Eureka moment!

In 1666, Isaac Newton discovered that white light is made up of different colours when he shone a beam of sunlight through a **prism**. A prism is a wedge of glass that refracts light and splits it into its different colours.

Why is the sky blue?

On a clear day, the sky looks blue because of the way the Earth's atmosphere scatters light from the Sun. As sunlight travels through the atmosphere towards Earth, it is scattered in all directions by gases and particles in the air. Blue light is scattered more than other colours because it travels as shorter, smaller waves. That's why we see blue sky most of the time. As the Sun gets lower in the sky, its light has to pass through more of the atmosphere to reach Earth. This means that more of the blue light is scattered, which lets other colours – the reds and yellows of a sunset – reach your eyes.

We see blue skies when particles in the atmosphere absorb and scatter more blue light than other colours.

Try this!

Raindrops and prisms can split white light into the seven colours of the rainbow. But did you know that you can reverse the process by mixing the seven colours together to make white light? You can find out how this is done by making a rainbow spinner.

What you need:

- white cardboard
- scissors
- a cup or jam jar
- a cork mat or mouse mat
- a piece of strong string about 120 centimetres (48 inches) long
- a protractor (optional)
- coloured pencils or felt tips in red, orange, yellow, green, blue, indigo, and violet
- a pencil

What you do

1. Use the cup or jam jar to draw a neat circle on the white card. Cut out this card circle.

2. Divide the circle into seven equal segments. (You can use the protractor to help you do this, if you know how.)

3 Colour the segments the seven colours of the rainbow: red, orange, yellow, green, blue, indigo, and violet.

4 Rest the card circle on the mat. Push a pencil through the card in two places to make two holes in the centre of the card about 1 centimetre (⅓ inch) apart.

5 Thread the string through the two holes and tie it so there is a loop at each end.

6 To spin your rainbow spinner, put one finger through the end of each loop and flip the disc over the string several times until the string has lots of twists in it. Pull your hands apart to tighten the string and then let the string go slack. If you do this properly, the disc should spin. What colour does the card look when it spins fast?

Stay safe!
Always ask an adult for help when using scissors and protractors.

Conclusion
When the disc is still, white light is reflected and absorbed by the different segments so we see separate rainbow colours. When the disc spins quickly, your brain does not have enough time to see the colours differently. Instead, it detects an overall mix of the colours, so the disc looks white or off-white.

How do we use light?

We use light in many different devices. We can use it to take photos, carry signals, and cut materials. By reflecting and refracting light in different ways, we can use it to see faraway objects and to make very tiny things visible.

Microscopes and telescopes

A compound microscope shines light through two sets of lenses to magnify very small objects on a slide in order to make them visible. A refracting telescope is a tube with a lens at each end. The first lens forms an image, and the second lens makes the image look bigger. In a reflecting telescope, the image is formed by reflection from a curved mirror that is then magnified by a second mirror.

Microscopes use lenses or mirrors to help us see tiny objects close up. Fifty of these tiny marine animals end to end would measure about 1 centimetre (1/3 inch).

Eureka moment!

In 1609, the Italian scientist Galileo made an improved version of previous attempts at making telescopes. His telescope boosted the viewing power enough for him to get a good look at the Moon.

Digital cameras

Digital cameras use light to make photos. Light enters the camera through a lens, as it does through an eye – but the light in the camera hits a sensor rather than a retina. The sensor detects the light and sends electrical signals to a microchip. The microchip processes and pieces together the information into an image that we can view on a screen.

This is the view a pilot has on a screen in the cockpit of an aeroplane when flying at night using a night-vision camera.

WHAT'S NEXT?

Night-vision goggles bounce infrared light (a type of light we cannot see) off a special screen to make a green or red image we can see. Previously, the screens were made from heavy glass and the goggles were expensive to produce. Scientists have found a way to construct much thinner goggles using cheap, lightweight plastic and other materials. In the future, the same technology might make night-vision spectacles and car windscreens commonplace.

Laser light

Laser is a special form of light that is made by machines. Laser light is made up of only one type of wavelength (or colour) of light. The light waves travel **parallel** to each other in the same direction, and do not scatter in the atmosphere. Laser beams are therefore very narrow, and can be concentrated on to one spot to produce a small point of intense energy. This makes lasers useful as cutting tools, as well as other things.

Eureka moment!

After their moonwalk in 1969, astronauts Buzz Aldrin and Neil Armstrong left a set of mirrors on the Moon. The mirrors reflect laser pulses sent from Earth so that scientists can precisely measure the distance from Earth to the Moon. We now know that the Moon is drifting 3.8 centimetres (1½ inches) away from Earth every year.

Some lasers are used to write and read CDs and DVDs.

Lasers can permanently change the shape of the cornea and improve patients' eyesight.

Using lasers

Lasers carry TV and telephone signals through special cables. Metal workers use lasers to cut and weld metal into a wide range of things, including cars. In clothing factories, lasers can cut through hundreds of layers of fabric at once. Lasers are also used in bar-code readers in shops. Because laser light travels in a straight line, it can be used for many types of alignment and measurement.

In surgery, lasers are sometimes used instead of scalpels because they can cut skin cleanly and precisely. They are especially useful in delicate eye surgery, where they are used to change the shape of the cornea so that it focuses light on the retina correctly.

WHAT'S NEXT?

Scientists have created a gadget that seals up flesh wounds with a quick zap of a laser. Could this be the end for surgical stitches?

How can we look after our eyes and ears?

Light and sound are vital to our lives, and it's important to protect our eyes and ears so we can go on using and experiencing light and sound as best we can.

Protecting ears

The loudness of sound is measure in decibels (dB). One decibel is the smallest sound we can hear. We speak at about 60 dB, and a clap of thunder can be 120 dB. Sounds of 85 dB or more can permanently damage ears – especially if they go on for a long time. It's important not to have the volume on your earphones set too loud, or stand too close to speakers at concerts.

People who work with noisy machinery for long periods protect their ears to avoid damaging their hearing.

DID YOU KNOW?

The sound of a jet aircraft taking off is about 120 dB. Pilots wear special headphones to protect their hearing. These headphones analyse the noise and then produce sound waves exactly opposite in shape that cancel out the noise of the aircraft.

Protecting eyes

The retinas in our eyes can be damaged by very bright light, so it's important to wear wide-brimmed hats and good-quality sunglasses on sunny days. Some people wear goggles to protect their eyes when playing sports. Wearing goggles when playing squash protects eyes from being hit by small, high-speed squash balls. Ski goggles prevent eye damage from sunlight reflecting off snow.

When we stare at a computer screen for a long time, we tend not to blink. This makes our eyes dry and tired, which is why we should take regular breaks and do something else. It is also vital to get regular check-ups at the opticians.

Eureka moment!

Inuit people made some of the earliest sunglasses from bone, leather, or wood with small slits to see through, to protect their eyes from the bright sunlight that reflects off snow.

Even when there's an exciting event like a solar eclipse — when the Moon passes in front of the Sun — we should *never* look directly towards the Sun.

Glossary

absorb take something in. For example, a sponge absorbs water.

acoustics way that sound travels in a confined space such as a room or theatre

atmosphere layer of gases that surround the Earth

bacteria living things that are too small to be seen without a microscope

concave curving in towards the centre

convex curving outwards on each side

echo sound caused by the reflection of sound waves from a surface back to the listener

echolocation way of finding objects and visualizing surroundings in the dark using reflected sound waves

electric current flow or movement of electricity

energy ability or power to do work

frequency number of vibrations per second

iris thin structure in eyes that controls how much light enters through the pupil and strikes the lens and retina inside. The iris is also the coloured part of the eye.

laser device that gives out a narrow, powerful beam of light, made up of a single wavelength or colour

lens in an eye, the clear part that focuses light rays on the retina. An artificial lens is a transparent object that refracts (bends) light in useful ways.

luminous gives out its own light

medium material through which sound or light waves can travel

mineral substance such as oil or metal that is found in the ground

nerves fibres that carry messages between the brain and the rest of the body, allowing us to do things such as see, hear, and feel pain.

opaque material through which light cannot pass

organ important body part such as the heart or liver

oxygen gas in the air that animals need to breathe in order to live

parallel when something is parallel to something else, they are side by side and have the same distance between them all the way along

particle extremely tiny piece of material

pitch how high or low a sound is

prism piece of glass with triangular ends that splits light into its separate colours

ray straight path or beam of light

reflect bend or throw back light

refraction the way light rays bend when they pass at an angle from one kind of material (such as water) to another (such as air)

retina layer at the back of the eyeball that is sensitive to light and sends signals to the brain about what we see

scattering when waves reflect or bounce off something in lots of different directions

sonar machine that uses the echoes of ultrasound waves to detect things under water or under ground

sound wave vibration in a medium such as air or water that we hear as sound

supersonic faster than the speed of sound

tumour mass of cells growing in a part of the body where they should not be

transparent material through which light passes easily, such as clear glass

translucent something that lets some but not all light pass through it

ultrasound high-frequency sound waves making sounds outside the range of normal human hearing

vacuum completely empty space with nothing in it, not even air

vibrate move forwards and backwards or to and fro, quickly and repeatedly

wavelength the distance between two crests of a wave

Find out more

Books

Investigating Light (Searchlight Books: How Does Energy Work?), Sally M. Walker (Lerner Classroom, 2011)

Investigating Sound (Searchlight Books: How Does Energy Work?), Sally M. Walker (Lerner Classroom, 2011)

Light (Science Detective Investigates), Katie Dicker (Wayland, 2011)

Sound (Science Detective Investigates), Harriet McGregor (Wayland, 2011)

Websites

www.bbc.co.uk/learningzone/clips/how-sound-waves-work-and-why-nothing-can-be-heard-in-a-vacuum/7913.html
Watch this clip to recap on how sound waves work and why nothing can be heard in a vacuum.

www.brainpopjr.com/science/energy/light/preview.weml
Learn more about light on this interactive website.

coolcosmos.ipac.caltech.edu
On this website, you can learn more about the amazing world of infrared and other wavelengths of light.

www.sciencekids.co.nz/projects/stringphone.html
Try making the string phone and other science experiments on this website.

Places to visit

The Science Museum
South Kensington
London
SW7 2DD

Explore the properties of light and sound in the hands-on
"Launchpad" gallery.

Glasgow Science Centre
50 Pacific Quay
Glasgow
G51 1EA

Visit the interactive science mall floors to experience light and sound
activities such as finding out what you look like as a thermal image.

Further research

Find out more about how a mirror reflects all the light that hits it to give
such good reflections. How do two-way mirrors work and where are
they useful?

Many animals use coloured patterns in their skin as camouflage. Cuttlefish,
octopuses, and chameleons are among those that can change colour as
they move across different-coloured backgrounds and to communicate.
Research how they do this.

A saxophone, an electric guitar, a trumpet, and a tabla drum make music
in different ways. Find out how each makes vibrations and what parts
make the sound louder. Then search for a piece of music featuring each
instrument that you like!

Index